M & GN

IN ACTION

First published 1981

ISBN 0 907087 04 3

BECKNELL BOOKS
P.O. BOX 21
KING'S LYNN
PE30 2QP

By the same authors:
M&GN IN FOCUS

Designed by Becknell Studio

Printed in Great Britain by Witley Press Ltd., Hunstanton

M & GN
IN ACTION

M. D. Beckett and P. R. Hemnell

BECKNELL BOOKS

NORWICH AND KING'S LYNN

Contents

Acknowledgements

In compiling this book we have received tremendous help from many people. We would like to thank especially: M. E. Back, Mrs. N. Back, D. H. Bayes, E. Blakey, GGS Photography, Norwich, R. C. Palmer, C. I. M. Shewring, R. J. Spinks, I. E. Watson, the staff of Witley Press Ltd, Hunstanton and A. C. Whittaker. The photographic credits are as follows: R. J. Adderson — 47, 66, 86, 92, 93, 94; Dr. Ian C. Allen — 15, 33, 40, Front cover; late E. L. Back collection — 29; C. S. Bayes — 5; A. E. Bennett — 34; H. C. Casserley — 43, 44, 52; R. E. Dean — 35; A. G. Ellis — 18, 49; Brian Fisher — 95; late T. G. Hepburn, courtesy Mrs. Hepburn — 16, 17, 21, 23, 25, 82, 85; H. N. James — 6, 8, 9, 19, 20, 22, 70, 80, 83, 103; K. A. Ladbury — 11; Lens of Sutton — 7, 50, 81; L&GRP collection, courtesy David & Charles — 1, 2, 3, 4; Lynn News & Advertiser — 32; Dr. W. J. Naunton — 67, 76; B. Reading — 71; L. R. Peters — 36, 38, 39, 53, 64, 69, 78, 98, 99, 100, 101, 104, Back cover; W. Stuart Sellar — 12; E. E. Smith, courtesy N. E. Stead — 31; C. R. Temple — 65; D. Thompson — 10; late E. Tuddenham, courtesy M&GN Circle — 28, 41, 45, 46, 48, 51, 55, 57, 59, 60, 61, 62, 63, 73, 77, 79, 84, 87, 89, 91, 96, 102; P. Waylett — 75, 88, 90; J. B. Westall — 14, 30, 42, 74; E. Woods — 26, 27, 97; G. A. Yeomans — 24, 37, 54, 56, 58, 68, 72. The photographer of photograph 13 is unknown. To all, our grateful thanks for capturing the M&GN on film while it was still there.

Organisations worth joining

Former M&GN employees, plus all those interested in the history of the Joint, should contact the M&GN Circle, 38 Holway Road, Sheringham, Norfolk. Those keen to see part of the M&GN preserved and kept in steam should get in touch with the M&GNJRS, Sheringham Station, Sheringham, Norfolk.

Front cover: 67386, King's Lynn shuttle at South Lynn.
Back cover: 43154, Runton West Junction, 1952.

Introduction

Although it was Britain's largest joint line, having a total length of 183 miles and services over a greater track mileage, the Midland & Great Northern never seemed to enjoy the same national esteem as the Somerset & Dorset Joint. Like all cross-country routes, the M&GN displayed a remarkable variety but perhaps the one thing its spirit of service didn't allow was any false sense of importance. Notwithstanding that, the *Joint* was dear to the hearts of many, as evidenced by the overwhelming response to our earlier book *M&GN In Focus.*

Conceived as a sequel to the previous album, this collection of photographs sets out to illustrate some of the amazing variety of the system. Of course, there was so much that it is impossible to show it all, but we hope some of its individuality will be recalled.

The locomotive policy was such that, in the early days, Midland designs prevailed (with the exception of one Great Northern freight class) and this trend was to continue, on and off, to the end. After the original Midland-inspired modernisation had taken place, the elderly 4-4-0s and 0-6-0s soldiered on until the LNER took over responsibility for the line in 1936. It is true the LMS loaned a handful of 2Ps just before the takeover, but the old *Joint* locos carried on giving sterling service until the LNER withdrew them in the face of its desire for standardisation. This simply didn't happen, for Stratford's regime saw Great Central, Great Northern and, inevitably, Great Eastern types at work over the system. It wasn't until after nationalisation that a degree of standardisation came in with the introduction of the foreign line's Ivatt 4MT 2-6-0s. Even that didn't end the variety!

Coaching stock exhibited the same diversity, ranging from ancient six-wheelers and second-hand bogies in M&GN days to old GE stock and Gresley teak later on with injections of LMS steel stock on through trains. These were always a fascinating feature. There were the two owning companies' services from their territories to the East Coast, M&GN trains running over the Midland as far as Leicester and Nottingham, and the Great Eastern's running powers (obtained at the cost of co-operation over constructing the N&SJR) to the *Joint* resort of Sheringham.

Business and holiday traffics were not the only ones to use this route from East Anglia to inland England. Freight — coal and merchandise in and fish, flowers, fruit and other arable produce (including sugar beet) out — was also very important in pre-road transport days. The traffics reflected the nature of the districts served: the East Midland vales, the vast levels of the Fens, rolling arable Norfolk, the coast, Poppyland, Broadland, quiet and noisy resorts and the commercial cities of Leicester, Norwich, Nottingham and Peterborough.

For the flatter part of Britain, there were several notable structures. At the western end, Lound Viaduct and Toft Tunnel were outstanding. Bridges were the main features in the Fens — criss-crossed by dykes and drains — those at Sutton Bridge and South Lynn being particularly noteworthy. But the largest bridge of all was at Yarmouth — at the other end of the M&GN. Built as a means of access to the southern section of the unique Norfolk & Suffolk Joint Railway, this magnificent five-span girder bridge — one span opened to allow passage to water craft — crossed the vast expanse of Breydon Water at the back of the town and was the system's largest engineering feature. The N&SJR system's claim to fame, apart from its separation into two district branches, was that it was the only British joint line to have a joint railway as joint owner!

The most remarkable Fenland location, though, was Murrow, where the *Joint* crossed another Joint — the GN&GEJR March-Spalding section — on the level. The foreign line was double and an interesting flat crossing resulted. Elsewhere, the line was less than level for, in central Norfolk, the terrain is surprisingly undulating and the line's builders were forced to choose some notably hilly alignments.

The 1950s saw the line at its most memorable and we have therefore concentrated largely on this period. It was often said that the biggest change came to the M&GN in 1936, when the LNER introduced new ways, and that nationalisation brought no real changes. Certainly the line was always known as the M&GN even in official BR literature, a testimony indeed to its sturdy independence. Perhaps its closure in February 1959 — the first complete main line to be axed — meant that the corporate identity of British Rail never reached it (with exceptions we mention below) but, more like, the tradition would have lived on. Certainly the diesels that did come had it: the Whitaker tablet catchers they were fitted with for the single line sections came off the steam locos they were replacing and were proudly stamped with the initials M&GN!

Parts of the line survived the main closure and reached the modern era. These too had their fascination, especially those, like the Sheringham-Melton branch and the Yarmouth South Town-Lowestoft section (upgraded to a main line upon the closure of the East Suffolk line's northern end and then downgraded to a single track branch) which continued for a few more years and then finally succumbed. We make no apology for illustrating this twilight period for, even if the motive power was functional and unglamorous, those days have passed into memory and will never be seen again.

Of course, the main reason for sections of the system surviving 1959 was freight and this is an aspect we have not overlooked either. Some of the interest disappeared when the Themelthorpe curve was laid between the GE and the Norwich line, saving hundreds of train miles at a stroke for no longer did freights from Norwich Thorpe to Norwich City have to go *round-the-world* via Cromer and Melton! Even so, for a distance of one mile direct, the rail journey was immense. Mention of Norwich City conjures up memories of its last years when, weed-infested and derelict as it all was, there was still sufficient freight traffic to require a pilot loco for the yard. Another freight line was the long siding from South Lynn to East Rudham — miles and miles of the former main line — used for the grain traffic until this ceased too. Freight continues on part of the Norwich line and at South Lynn and the Cromer-Sheringham section still has a daily passenger service, but that is all that is left in the ownership of BR. The North Norfolk Railway preserves a further three miles.

The M&GN was at its busiest on a summer Saturday and that is how it is best remembered, preferably in the 1950s when quantities of 4F 0-6-0s would be arriving at South Lynn to hand over their packed holiday trains to the *Joint's* 4MT 2-6-0s. Echoes indeed of the old tradition of elderly M&GN 4-4-0 relieving double-headed Midland trains there. That is how we hope it will be recalled. Critics nicknamed it the *Muddle and Get Nowhere* but many would disagree, claiming it is *Missed and Greatly Needed!* Thanks to its many photographers, it still lives on.

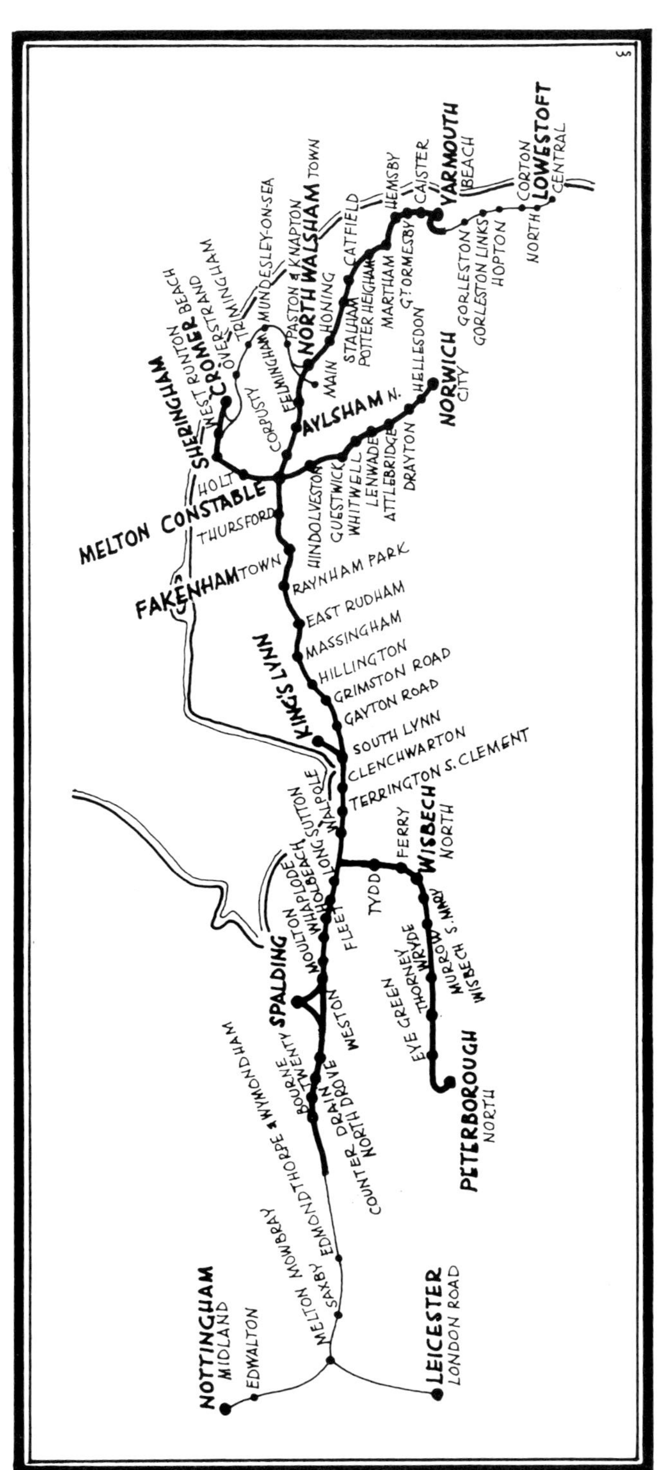

NOTTINGHAM
MIDLAND
EDWALTON
MELTON MOWBRAY
SAXBY
EDMONDTHORPE & WYMONDHAM
LEICESTER
LONDON ROAD
BOURNE
TWENTY
SPALDING
COUNTER DRAIN
NORTH DROVE
WESTON
MOULTON
WHAPLODE
HOLBEACH
FLEET
LONG SUTTON
WALPOLE
TYDD
SUTTON BRIDGE
EYE GREEN
THORNEY
WRYDE
MURROW
WISBECH S. MARY
PETERBOROUGH
NORTH
FERRY
WISBECH
NORTH
TERRINGTON S. CLEMENT
CLENCHWARTON
SOUTH LYNN
GAYTON ROAD
GRIMSTON ROAD
HILLINGTON
MASSINGHAM
EAST RUDHAM
RAYNHAM PARK
KING'S LYNN
FAKENHAM TOWN
THURSFORD
HOLT
MELTON CONSTABLE
HINDOLVESTON
GUESTWICK
WHITWELL
LENWADE
ATTLEBRIDGE
DRAYTON
HELLESDON
NORWICH
CITY
AYLSHAM N.
CORPUSTY
SHERINGHAM
WEST RUNTON
CROMER
BEACH
OVERSTRAND
TRIMINGHAM
MUNDESLEY-ON-SEA
FELMINGHAM
PASTON & KNAPTON
NORTH WALSHAM TOWN
HONING
MAIN
STALHAM
CATFIELD
POTTER HEIGHAM
MARTHAM
HEMSBY
G.T. ORMESBY
CAISTER
YARMOUTH
BEACH
GORLESTON
GORLESTON LINKS
HOPTON
CORTON
NORTH
LOWESTOFT
CENTRAL

MAP OF THE
MIDLAND AND GREAT NORTHERN JOINT RAILWAY
AND ASSOCIATED LINES

Through trains

1. Great Northern through trains ran from King's Cross to Cromer, changing locos at Peterborough. Gresley K2 2-6-0 1702 is seen at Holme on a returning Cromer excursion in 1922.

2. The LMS introduced a Gloucester-Lowestoft train in summer 1924. Midland 2P 4-4-0 431 nears the summit of the Lickey at Blackwell with this service one year later.

3. By 1939, when LMS *Crab* 2-6-0 2824 was seen on the train at Churchdown, the Gloucester coaches were attached to the *Leicester* along with West Riding ones.

4. This 1922 view of Holden B12 4-6-0 1532 on an up Great Eastern Sheringham express at Gidea Park would not have been possible but for the GER's 1897 running powers.

Peterborough

5. Peterborough North was mainly the interchange for the GN, although the Midland was represented. 4-4-0 76, in the later chocolate livery, runs light through the station on 21st May 1934.

6. Some passenger services ran from Peterborough North right through to Yarmouth Beach. The Ivatt 4MTs were the line's mainstay in later days. 43111 awaits departure in August 1952.

7. Earlier times are recalled by Johnson class C 4-4-0 77, a pure Midland design, bringing its train of typically ancient six-wheelers to journey's end at Peterborough North.

8. Railways rarely change greatly as this 1952 scene at the same location shows! 4MT 2-6-0 43082 brings an up M&GN fast to its destination past 43058 on a GN working.

9. Spital Bridge MR, East LNER and, finally, New England LNER were the Peterborough sheds used. J4 0-6-0 64160 — M&GN 85, *uniquely* numbered by BR — was at the latter in 1951.

10. The rural face of the line is amply illustrated by this peaceful summer scene of Peterborough-bound LNER J4 0-6-0 4154 halted at Wisbech St. Mary station.

11. Ivatt J6 0-6-0 64177, formerly 528 of the class known on the Great Northern as *A engines*, trundles a freight through Wisbech North's picturesque platforms on 5th August 1958.

12. The peaceful tranquillity at Wisbech North is disturbed by 4MT 2-6-0 43147 pulling away with a three-coach stopping passenger for Peterborough North on 30th September 1958.

13. Passing Wisbech North Yard, class C 4-4-0 13 brings up express duty 23 over Leverington Road crossing at Wisbech, having just entered the double-track section extending to the station.

14. Sutton Bridge was where the Peterborough route met that from Spalding and the west. An unidentified Ivatt 4MT hurries round the curve off the Peterborough road at the junction.

15. South Lynn's 43142 brings a westbound train of Stanier LMS stock over the Nene at Sutton Bridge. The bridge, once half rail and half road, sadly now carries the latter only.

Midland feeders

16. Foreign locos regularly came onto the *Joint* but M&GN classes ventured afield themselves, for example on the Spalding-Nottingham service. Beyer Peacock class A 4-4-0 22 stands at Nottingham Midland.

17. Still on the Midland, M&GN class C 4-4-0 53 is seen piloting an unidentified LMS 2-6-4T on a Nottingham Midland-Yarmouth Beach train in Edwalton cutting, just south of Nottingham.

18. The cross-country route to Leicester was the M&GN's backbone, although the section from Little Bytham to Leicester was totally Midland owned. 4-4-0 45 reaches Leicester London Road.

19. Summarising the *Joint's* nature is this rare 1937 shot of LMS 4F 0-6-0 3937 piloting LNER ex-Great Central D9 4-4-0 6018 at Leicester on a freight bound for the M&GN.

20. The M&GN route diverged at Saxby, though was Midland property as far as Little Bytham. 2-6-4T 42184 and 4F 0-6-0 44419 share the 9.55 a.m. Derby-Gorleston on 26th July 1958.

21. Another 4F brings a returning Yarmouth-Derby train through Edmondthorpe & Wymondham, its number obscured by the train number board; holiday traffic needed strict control over the single line.

22. A busy time at Saxby on 26th July 1958. 4F 0-6-0 43937 enters the station with the 9 a.m. Leicester-Yarmouth, passing a three-coach local. The 4F carries control number 55.

23. Shortly after the 1936 LNER takeover, Robinson D9 4-4-0s were introduced to replace the ageing M&GN locos on the expresses. 6040 is just west of Toft Tunnel with the up *Leicester*.

24. Johnson Midland 2P 4-4-0 40454 of Nottingham shed stands at Bourne's lengthy island platform in July 1953, ready to depart with the 4.21 p.m. King's Lynn-Nottingham semi-fast.

25. How many stations between Bourne and Spalding? Of course, two — and *Twenty* — where Gresley J6 0-6-0 64231 of Boston shed is seen with a Bourne-Spalding pick-up freight.

26. 43080 brings an eastbound excursion off the Spalding avoiding line, built in 1894 to avoid reversal of through trains. The station line is seen diverging under the sixth coach.

27. A westbound excursion of LMS stock, control reporting number M106, is hauled by 4F 0-6-0 44034 of Leicester Midland shed, seen crossing the Welland girder bridge at Spalding.

28. An unidentified 4MT 2-6-0 enters Holbeach from the east with a flower train, recalling the vast South Holland horticultural traffics. The platform barrows are loaded with flower boxes.

29. On closure day, 28th February 1959, J6 0-6-0 64172 heads the 9.55 a.m. ex Saxby stopping passenger towards Long Sutton, where it will form the 11.15 a.m. departure.

30. Sutton Bridge was an interesting station having one road served by two platform faces, a feature repeated at South Lynn. 43155, however, stands at the outer up platform.

31. The present Cross Keys swingbridge at Sutton Bridge was opened on 28th July 1897, the swing span being 176 feet long. This westbound passenger is hauled by an unidentified J6.

32. Another bridge, that over the Ouse at South Lynn, was claimed to be in such bad repair that it ensured the line's closure. 43158 is seen with the very last westbound *Leicester*.

33. *Yorkie* J4 0-6-0 4154 climbs away from South Lynn with a marvellously assorted rake bound for Sutton Bridge. The scene is pre-war, probably dating around 1938.

The King's Lynn shuttle

34. Originally operating into King's Lynn over a soon-abandoned line, the M&GN introduced a shuttle service from South Lynn. N7 0-6-2T 69698 awaits departure on 14th February 1959.

35. The C12 4-4-2Ts, typified by 67374, were more usual power. South Lynn was poorly sited for King's Lynn and the shuttle connected with trains lacking through Lynn coaches.

36. The same loco has just arrived at South Lynn on 1st August 1953. 4F 0-6-0 44158 has just relieved a 4MT 2-6-0 on an up passenger and is receiving its train reporting number board.

37. Another of this Ivatt GN 4-4-2T class, 67386, stands at King's Lynn M&GN platform 5 on 6th September 1957. *Joint* trains also used number 1 on the down side.

38. Having brought eastbound train M69 in from Leicester on Saturday 16th August 1952, 4F 0-6-0 43937 will be detached for servicing at South Lynn and replaced by 4MT 2-6-0 43156.

39. Sister 4MT 43155 of Melton Constable makes a spirited start out of South Lynn on the same day with a stopping passenger, a contrast in duties for this versatile and universal class.

40. Surprisingly perhaps, the M&GN never had any of the standard Fowler 4F 0-6-0s of its own. However, it had sixteen of the earlier Johnson type, 62 being seen near Massingham.

41. Ivatt 4MT 2-6-0 43148 coasts downhill past Massingham Air Ministry Siding on 26th August 1958 with the 2.46 p.m. Melton Constable-South Lynn class J freight.

42. Fakenham West No. 1 box, past which 43154 brings the 2.48 p.m. to Peterborough, was actually at the eastern end of the station, known in M&GN days as Fakenham Town.

43. Twelve of a batch of thirty-five GN Ivatt 0-6-0s were obtained for the M&GN in 1900. On 4th July 1936 no. 86 of the class was seen near Thursford, climbing the 1 in 100 Thursford bank.

44. Robinson D9 4-4-0 6041, one of the type known on the M&GN as *Puggies*, makes a fine exhaust as it pulls out of Melton Constable on 13th March 1939, heading towards Fakenham.

45. Nineteen years later — on 10th March 1958 — 4MT 43161 leaves Melton after a snowstorm with the *Leicester*, the combined 9.2 a.m. ex Yarmouth and the 9.40 a.m. ex Cromer to Birmingham.

46. Hill J19 0-6-0 64654 passes Melton West box in this May 1953 view, heading tender-first out onto the main line with the breakdown train. The Cromer road is behind the box.

47. Six years later, Melton became a mere branch-line terminus. Near the end of its days thus — on Easter Monday 30th March 1964 — the 4 p.m. to Norwich Thorpe passes Melton West.

48. This view from Melton East box shows an unidentified Brush Type 2 A1A-A1A diesel, now class 31, leaving on a *round-the-world* freight for Norwich City before the opening of the Themelthorpe curve.

49. Although Norfolk is largely arable, cattle nevertheless travelled frequently by rail in earlier days. Johnson class C 4-4-0 no. 1 stands on a cattle train at Melton on 26th May 1934.

50. Another cattle train is headed by class A 4-4-0 24, also at Melton. Comparison can readily be made between this 1882 design and the M&GN mainstay, Johnson's class C of 1894.

51. Holden J17 0-6-0 65586 stands at the eastern end of Melton Constable with a southbound freight. The slotted concrete post is a reminder of the Joint's pioneering use of this material.

52. Evidence of the variety seen at Melton is Ivatt D2 4-4-0 4322 seen on 28th May 1937. The LNER put this class on most of the Norwich line work for a few years.

53. The LNER also introduced the ex-GE Holden *Claud Hamilton* 4-4-0s. D16/3 62533 is seen at Melton MPD with Ivatt 4MT 2-6-0 43150. This shed scene is dated 15th June 1952.

54. This beautiful photograph shows sister *Claud Hamilton* D16/3 4-4-0 62561 posing for the camera on the Melton Constable seventy foot vacuum-operated turntable in September 1957.

55. Four *standard* 4MT 2-6-0s were fitted with tablet catchers but were never sent to the M&GN. However, 76034 went to Norwich Thorpe and ventured to Melton on a Norwich City freight.

56. D16/3 4-4-0 62519 of Melton Constable stands there in September 1956 at the head of a train of Stanier LMS stock. The single-lamp headcode would suggest this train is a local!

57. Worsdell J15 0-6-0 65469 hauls a class 1 engineers train, including the beautiful Norwich DCE saloon, near Melton East on 24th May 1960, over a year after the main closure.

58. July 1954 and Holden F6 2-4-2T 67225 was acting on pilot duty at Melton Constable. The large glazed cabs resulted in the popular class nickname of *Glasshouse Gobblers*.

59. 65581, a Holden J17 0-6-0, passes Melton East in charge of a summer Saturday passenger train on 24th August 1957. The upper-quadrant board contrasts with the usual GN somersaults.

60. Gresley K2 2-6-0 61748 passes Themelthorpe, later site of the British Railways curve to the old GER branch, on 10th May 1949 with the 12.45 p.m. class B South Lynn-Norwich City freight.

61. D16/3 4-4-0 62597 shuts off steam at the summit for the 1 in 100 descent to Whitwell & Reepham with the 1.32 p.m. Melton Constable-Norwich City on 25th May 1957.

62. Making a superb exhaust over the flat arable landscape, J17 0-6-0 65509 is seen near Whitwell & Reepham with the 3.36 p.m. Norwich City-South Lynn freight on 3rd May 1950.

63. Gresley J39 0-6-0 64968 enters Drayton heading for Norwich City with the breakdown crane on a line-clearing job, whilst another J39 awaits the right-of-way to Lenwade.

64. *Buckjumper* J69 0-6-0T 68623 was seen at Norwich City on 18th June 1952. This well-travelled former Great Eastern suburban tank had just been transferred from St. Margaret's, Edinburgh!

65. A *Derby lightweight* dmu stands at Norwich City awaiting departure for Cromer Beach on 20th February 1959. After the bombing of 27/28 April 1942 the terminus always looked semi-derelict.

66. Metro-Cammell dmus, forming the 2.5 p.m. Melton-Norwich Thorpe, left, and the 12.59 p.m. Norwich-Melton, make the very last daylight crossing at Holt on the branch closure day, 4th April 1964.

67. A hot summer day in August 1955 and 4MT 2-6-0 43154 takes its freight out of Weybourne on the 1 in 80 climb to Kelling, well-known as the prettiest part of the whole M&GN system!

68. The school train, the 4.17 p.m. from North Walsham Main, reaches the end of its journey at Sheringham number 2 platform in September 1957. Thompson B1 4-6-0 61270 is in charge.

69. East Runton viaduct saw D16/3 4-4-0 62584 heading towards Cromer Beach on 20th June 1952. The viaduct on the left carried the N&S route towards Overstrand and Mundesley.

70. Passing the site of Gas Works Siding at Runton East Junction, Thompson B1 4-6-0 61043 hauls a freight tender-first out of Cromer Beach towards Sheringham and Melton in August 1961.

71. Now preserved on the North Norfolk Railway at Sheringham, Gresley B12/3 — a derivation of the S.D. Holden design — 4-6-0 61572 has just been turned on the Cromer Beach sixty-five foot table.

72. Standing in the terminus in July 1954 was B17 4-6-0 61665 *Leicester City* with a Sheringham train. Cromer Beach is still noted today for its elegant overall roof, although barricaded and in private use.

73. The 1.10 p.m. Sheringham-Norwich Thorpe was routed via the N&S Mundesley loop. On 6th April 1953, D16/3 4-4-0 62617 was in charge as it left Trimmingham's simplified station layout.

74. The Norfolk Railway Society was noted for hiring the Mundesley branch on a Sunday for engine-driving practice! Passengers are rung aboard 65469's train with the original N&SJR handbell.

75. Schools traffic was very important in the rural areas as the bicycles at Mundesley-on-Sea testify. The scholars from North Walsham leave the Metro-Cammell two-car dmu to head for home.

76. N7/3 0-6-2T 69698, fitted for push-pull, propels the 4.5 p.m. ex North Walsham Main into Mundesley on 11th August 1955, past the biggest grouping of camping coaches on British Railways.

Melton Constable to Yarmouth Beach

77. 4MTs cross at Aylsham North in 1958. 43091 stands on the 6.54 a.m. Peterborough North-Yarmouth Beach as 43158 enters with the 9.2 a.m. Yarmouth-Birmingham New Street *Leicester*.

78. North Walsham Town was actually in sight of the Great Eastern's *Main* establishment. The rival concern, in the shape of *Claud Hamilton* D16/3 62564, stands at Town on 19th June 1952.

79. 43158 heads the 10.38 a.m. Caister-on-Sea to Liverpool Street *Holiday Camps Express* near Honing on 13th July 1957. This summer Saturdays train will reverse onto the GE at North Walsham.

80. The 1 p.m. Stalham-Yarmouth Beach enters Martham on closure day, 28th February 1959, behind 4MT 43160. This loco later left redundant Yarmouth Beach with sister 43157, light to Melton Constable.

81. Passing the lovely enamel Great Yarmouth Beach Station nameboard is Gresley D3 4-4-0 4355. This class was rebuilt between 1912 and 1928 from an Ivatt Great Northern 1896 design.

82. Sitting in the bay platform at Yarmouth Beach waiting for the *off* is Ivatt C12 4-4-2T 4502 with a Lowestoft Central local, formed of six-wheelers and just one solitary bogie.

83. Closure day again: 28th February 1959. 4MT 2-6-0 43107, which later took out one of the last freights, stands on the shed road about noon. 43157 lurks almost hidden in the shed.

84. The largest structure on the M&GN was the 800 feet long Breydon Viaduct. Four spans were fixed and one swung, distinguishable by the control tower. A 2-4-2T heads towards Gorleston and Lowestoft.

85. Gorleston Links Halt was opened in July 1914 to serve the adjacent course. Pollitt MS&LR F2 2-4-2T 5781 pauses there wrong road with a two-coach Lowestoft local in LNER days.

86. There are plenty of passengers to board the 2.21 p.m. Lowestoft Central-Yarmouth South Town on 2nd May 1970. Sadly, this Cravens dmu set was working the closure day journeys.

87. J15 0-6-0 65472 pulls out of Lowestoft Central tender-first with the 12.15 p.m. Yarmouth South Town departure on 9th September 1957. The N&S route diverged at Coke Ovens Junction.

88. Several specials traversed M&GN metals following closure to passenger traffic. The M&GNJRPS, as it was then sponsored a tour on 8th October 1960. Now-preserved B12/3 4-6-0 61572 is seen at Norwich.

89. A similar special with J15 0-6-0 65469 at Melton Constable on 21st May 1960. The Melton-Sheringham service was still operating with diesels and did not cease until April 1964.

90. The fourth M&GNJRPS special ran on 26th May 1962 from Cambridge to East Rudham — via Stoke Ferry! 4MT 43149, back in its old haunts, is seen with the up working near Massingham.

91. A *Trains Illustrated* enthusiasts' excursion in the hands of Thompson B1 4-6-0 61113 coasts under the A148 road bridge on the Norfolk & Suffolk section near Cromer in August 1959.

Freight after 1959

92. Freight services lasted on the Norwich and the South Lynn-East Rudham lines for many years. D5867 shunts Pointer's sand train over Drayton A-frame bridge on 23rd April 1969.

93. After the 1960 opening of Themelthorpe curve, Norwich Thorpe-Norwich City freights no longer had to go *round-the-world* via Cromer. D5579 shunts Drayton Yard on 14th April 1969.

94. Grassgrown sidings show what had happened at Norwich City as D5545, in the then new blue livery, arrives with the morning freight on 4th June 1968. The Norwich A-frame bridge is beyond.

95. D5631 enters a derelict Grimston Road with a returning East Rudham-South Lynn grain train. There were three brake vans on 17th February 1968 for a special Norfolk Railway Society party.

Loco variety

96. As befits a joint line, the loco variety was tremendous. Earlier days reflected LMS and LNER ownership but the 1950s offered more: *Austerity* 2-8-0 90280 at Melton East in September 1960.

97. J6 0-6-0 4207 and D3 4-4-0 62131 take the afternoon Nottingham train out of Spalding just after the 1948 nationalisation. The pilot still carries its LNER number whilst the 4-4-0 is BR-liveried.

98. Interestingly, several Great Central classes came with the LNER takeover as Robinson *Pom-Pom* J11 0-6-0 64420, seen on 1st August 1953 setting out eastwards from South Lynn, demonstrates.

99. Yet the Midland influence carried on to the end: 4F 0-6-0s 44423, 43937 and 44412, having turned and watered at South Lynn, wait there to take over from 4MTs coming in from Yarmouth.

100. The 4Fs did venture east but the general atmosphere was more LNER. Gresley V1 2-6-2T 67679 is at Runton West Junction on 18th June 1951 with the down Sheringham portion of the *Broadsman*.

101. East Runton is the location too for this charming shot of F4 2-4-2T 67225 on a N&S route local dated 20th June 1952. Three of the four bogies are vintage Great Eastern stock!

102. But the workhorses were undisputedly the Ivatt 4MT 4-6-0s. 43158 is seen passing Gayton Road up starter — a beautiful product of the S&T Dept. — with the westbound *Leicester*.

End of the line

103. Stratford took over the Loco Dept. in 1936, supervising heavy repairs — and most scrapping. Wartime arrivals, though, sometimes saw emergency GE use, Enfield and Romford both seeing *Joint* locos.

104. Dating from 1903, Marriott's Melton Constable-built 0-6-0T 8488, formerly M&GN 2A then 94, was on its way to Stratford for breaking in 1948 when it was seen in Cambridge Yard.